A Li...
of God's W...

Written and Compiled by
Clift Richards & Lloyd Hildebrand

Victory House, Inc.
Tulsa, Oklahoma

A LITTLE BIT OF GOD'S WISDOM AND WIT
Copyright © 1994 by K & C International, Inc.
ISBN: 0-932081-42-8
Printed in the United States of America

Published by Victory House, Inc.
P.O. Box 700238
Tulsa, Oklahoma 74170
(918) 747-5009

Cover Design by : *Whitley Graphics*

INTRODUCTION

It is our hope that you will find this book to be a treasury of timely truths that you can apply to your daily life. Some of the quotations and insights will make you laugh; others will make you look squarely at the issues of your life and relationships. We hope that these pearls of wisdom will brighten your day, change your life in positive ways, and bring enlightenment and hope to your heart.

From the Bible, you will listen to the words of Jesus, Paul, the prophets, and the apostles. In many cases, their words will coincide with the statements of Ben Franklin, Mark Twain, Charles Hadden Spurgeon, Peter Marshall, Abraham Lincoln and others. All of their affirmations lead us to incorporate timely wisdom into our thinking and living and to find the way to greater productivity, health, hope, and accomplishment.

The writer of the Proverbs describes the purpose and impact of inspired words: "A word fitly spoken is like apples of gold in pictures of silver" (Proverbs 25:11). We trust that you will enjoy these "apples of gold," and we know that they will shine even more brightly as you take a moment to ponder their meaning for your life.

TO OUR READERS

If you have favorite humorous or wise sayings or anecdotes that we could include in future books, please send them to:

Clift Richards & Lloyd Hildebrand
c/o Victory House, Inc.
P.O. Box 700238
Tulsa, OK 74170

OTHER BOOKS OF INTEREST

A Little Bit of God's Wisdom and Wit
A Little Bit of God's Wisdom and Wit for Men
A Little Bit of God's Wisdom and Wit for Women
Prayers That Prevail — The Believer's Manual of Prayers
Prayers That Prevail for America — Changing a Nation Through Prayer
Prayers That Prevail for Your Children — A Parent's and Grandparent's
    Manual of Prayers

All titles are available at your local
bookstore or through Victory House, Inc.

I am oftimes driven to my knees by the overwhelming conviction that I have nowhere else to go.

(Abraham Lincoln)

The prayer of a righteous man is powerful and effective
(James 5:16, NIV).

Don't give yourself "the benefit of the doubt" — doubt has no benefits.

He that wavereth is like a wave of the sea driven with the wind (James 1:6).

Our capacity in spiritual matters is measured by the promises of God.

(Oswald Chambers)

For all the promises of God in Him are Yes, and in Him Amen, to the glory of God through us (2 Corinthians 1:20, NKJV).

The grass is always greener on the other side of the fence — until you get there.

---◆•◆---

For I have learned, in whatsoever state I am, therewith to be content (Philippians 4:11).

God loves you!

For God so loved the world, that he gave his only begotten Son, that whosoever believeth in him should not perish, but have everlasting life (John 3:16).

Real faith never goes home with an empty basket.

If you have faith as a mustard seed, you will say to this mountain, 'Move from here to there,' and it will move; and nothing will be impossible for you (Matthew 17:20, NKJV).

Joy is the echo of God's life within us.

(Joseph Marmion)

The joy of the Lord is your strength (Nehemiah 8:10).

The happiness of your life depends on the quality of your thoughts.

For as he thinketh in his heart, so is he (Proverbs 23:7).

Sin is my claim to my right to myself.

(Oswald Chambers)

Whatsoever is not of faith is sin (Romans 14:23).

The higher a man is in grace, the lower he will be in his own esteem

(Charles H. Spurgeon)

◆●◆

Let nothing be done through strife or vainglory; but in lowliness of mind let each esteem other better than themselves (Philippians 2:3).

Love's first response is to give.

Freely ye have received, freely give (Matthew 10:8).

The sweetest lesson I have learned in God's school is to let the Lord choose for me.

(Dwight L. Moody)

The Lord will perfect that which concerneth me: thy mercy, O Lord, endureth for ever: forsake not the works of thine own hands (Psalm 138:8).

Take time to laugh. It is the music of the soul.

A merry heart doeth good like a medicine: but a broken spirit drieth the bones (Proverbs 17:22).

A crossless life means a crownless death.

Be thou faithful unto death, and I will give thee a crown of life (Revelations 2:10).

God can do anything but fail.

Is any thing too hard for the Lord? (Genesis 18:14).

Worry comes when human beings interfere with God's plan.

—◆•◆—

Casting all your care upon him; for he careth for you (1 Peter 5:7).

God gives by promises so that we may receive by faith.

Imitate those who through faith and patience inherit the promises (Hebrews 6:12, NKJV).

It is not how much of God we have that counts, but how much of us does God have?

For it is God which worketh in you both to will and to do of his good pleasure (Philippians 2:13).

A genuine faith sings songs in the darkest night.

❖

And call upon me in the day of trouble: I will deliver thee, and thou shalt glorify me (Psalm 50:15).

The real secret of prayer is praying in secret.

Ask, and it shall be given you; seek, and ye shall find; knock, and it shall be opened unto you (Matthew 7:7).

Forgiveness is the fragrance the violet sheds on the heel that has crushed it.

(Mark Twain)

Forbearing one another, and forgiving one another, if any man have a quarrel against any: even as Christ forgave you, so also do ye (Colossians 3:13).

If you were arrested for being a Christian, would there be enough evidence to convict you?

For to me to live is Christ, and to die is gain (Philippians 1:21).

God loves a cheerful giver — until he brags about it.

Every man according as he purposeth in his heart, so let him give; not grudgingly, or of necessity: for God loveth a cheerful giver (2 Corinthians 9:7).

A memory stored with Scripture is a bank that will never fail.

Thy word have I hid in mine heart, that I might not sin against thee (Psalm 119:11).

The heart that loves is always young.

Let us hold fast the profession of our faith without wavering; (for he is faithful that promised;) And let us consider one another to provoke unto love and to good works (Hebrews 10:23-24).

Who hath God hath all; who hath Him not, hath less than nothing.

(Ancient proverb)

———◆•◆———

For in him we live, and move, and have our being (Acts 17:28).

Circumstances are not your master.

For in him we live, and move, and have our being; as certain also of your own poets have said, For we are also his offspring (Acts 17:28).

To have a friend, be a friend.

A friend loves at all times, And a brother is born for adversity (Proverbs 17:17, NKJV).

Invest your time in the most important things of life.

◆——●——◆

You did not choose me, but I chose you and appointed you to go and bear fruit — fruit that will last. Then the Father will give you whatever you ask in my name. This is my command: Love each other (John 15:16–17, NIV).

Wisdom isn't the acquisition of knowledge, rather it is knowing which knowledge is worth acquiring.

Happy is the man that findeth wisdom, and the man that getteth understanding (Proverbs 3:13).

The way up is down.

———◆-◆———

Humble yourselves therefore under the mighty hand of God, that he may exalt you in due time (1 Peter 5:6).

One day at a time.

Take therefore no thought for the morrow: for the morrow shall take thought for the things of itself. Sufficient unto the day is the evil thereof (Matthew 6:34).

Many people mistake our work for our vocation. Our vocation is the love of Jesus.

(Mother Teresa)

───◆•◆───

He that loveth me not keepeth not my sayings (John 14:24).

What you do in secret reveals the content of your character.

———◆•◆———

Who can understand his errors? cleanse thou me from secret faults (Psalm 19:12).

Confession is good for the soul and for the body.

Therefore confess your sins to each other and pray for each other so that you may be healed. The prayer of a righteous man is powerful and effective (James 5:16, NIV).

If you think you're not conceited, it means you are very conceited indeed.

(C.S. Lewis)

But he giveth more grace. Wherefore he saith, God resisteth the proud, but giveth grace unto the humble (James 4:6).

40

The religion of Jesus begins with the verb "follow" and ends with the word "go."

And he saith unto them, Follow me, and I will make you fishers of men (Matthew 4:19).

Faith is the mouth which feeds on Christ.

(Charles Haddon Spurgeon)

The word is nigh thee, even in thy mouth (Romans 10:8).

Faith is obedient; it goes when commanded.

(E.M. Bounds)

According to your faith be it unto you (Matthew 9:29).

Jesus is the Master Controller of all things.

◆•◆

For by him were all things created, that are in heaven, and that are in earth, visible and invisible, whether they be thrones, or dominions, or principalities, or powers: all things were created by him, and for him: And he is before all things, and by him all things consist (Colossians 1:16-17).

Spiritual investments reap eternal dividends.

———◆•◆———

But lay up for yourselves treasures in heaven....For where your treasure is, there will your heart be also (Matthew 6:20–21).

You are the apple of God's eye.

Keep me as the apple of the eye, hide me under the shadow of thy wings (Psalm 17:8).

Put God first.

But seek ye first the kingdom of God, and his righteousness; and all these things shall be added unto you (Matthew 6:33).

Reflect upon your present blessings — not on your past misfortunes.

(Charles Dickens)

Rejoice evermore (1 Thessalonians 5:16).

Practice the presence of God.

Come near to God and he will come near to you (James 4:8, NIV).

If you judge people, you have no time to love them.

(Mother Theresa)

———◆•◆———

And walk in love, as Christ also has loved us and given Himself for us, an offering and a sacrifice to God for a sweet-smelling aroma (Ephesians 5:2, NKJV).

God is not finished with you yet.

❖•❖

For we are his workmanship, created in Christ Jesus unto good works, which God hath before ordained that we should walk in them (Ephesians 2:10).

God hears and answers your prayers.

---◆•◆---

And this is the confidence that we have in him, that, if we ask any thing according to his will, he heareth us: And if we know that he hear us, whatsoever we ask, we know that we have the petitions that we desired of him (1 John 5:14-15).

His [God's] promise is a threefold cord that cannot be broken.

(Andrew Murray)

◆•◆

And all things, whatsoever ye shall ask in prayer, believing, ye shall receive (Matthew 21:22).

I believe that love is stronger than death.

(Robert Fulghum)

———◆•◆———

There is no fear in love; but perfect love casteth out fear: because fear hath torment. He that feareth is not made perfect in love (1 John 4:18).

The Christian has no law but Christ.

(Thomas Merton)

Bear ye one another's burdens, and so fulfill the law of Christ (Galatians 6:2).

Choose life!

I have set before you life and death, blessing and cursing: therefore choose life, that both thou and thy seed may live (Deuteronomy 30:19).

Unless the Spirit fills, the spirit fails.

But if the Spirit of him that raised up Jesus from the dead dwell in you, he that raised up Christ from the dead shall also quicken your mortal bodies by his Spirit that dwelleth in you (Romans 8:11).

Christianity is the land of beginning again.

(W.A. Criswell)

And he that sat upon the throne said, Behold, I make all things new (Revelation 21:5).

Let your heart be broken with the things that break the heart of God.

———◆•◆———

Is not this the fast that I have chosen? to loose the bands of wicked-ness, to undo the heavy burdens, and to let the oppressed go free, and that ye break every yoke? (Isaiah 58:6).

The waters are rising, but so am I. I am not going under, but over.

(Catherine Booth)

When the enemy shall come in like a flood, the Spirit of the Lord shall lift up a standard against him (Isaiah 59:19).

Work as if everything depended upon your work, and pray as if everything depended on your prayer.

(William Booth)

———◆•◆———

Rejoice evermore. Pray without ceasing. In every thing give thanks: for this is the will of God in Christ Jesus concerning you (1 Thessalonians 5:16–18).

The door to your heart can be opened only from the inside.

Behold, I stand at the door, and knock: if any man hear my voice, and open the door, I will come in to him, and will sup with him, and he with me (Revelation 3:20).

Become better, not bitter.

———◆•◆———

Looking diligently lest any man fail of the grace of God; lest any root of bitterness springing up trouble you, and thereby many be defiled (Hebrews 12:15).

Where you go hereafter depends on what you go after here.

For the wages of sin is death; but the gift of God is eternal life through Jesus Christ our Lord (Romans 6:23).

There are two kinds of people in the world: those who brighten the room when they enter, and those who brighten the room when they leave.

That you may become blameless and harmless, children of God without fault in the midst of a crooked and perverse generation, among whom you shine as lights in the world (Philippians 2:15, NKJV).

When it is hardest to pray, it is time to pray hardest.

————◆•◆————

*In my distress I cried unto the Lord, and he heard me
(Psalm 120:1).*

If you are too busy to pray, you are too busy.

◆•◆

Call unto me, and I will answer thee, and show thee great and mighty things, which thou knowest not (Jeremiah 33:3).

The best revenge is to ignore the wrong.

◆•◆

Blessed are you, when they revile and persecute you, and say all kinds of evil against you falsely for My sake. Rejoice, and be exceedingly glad, for great is your reward in heaven, for so they persecuted the prophets who were before you (Matthew 5:11–12, NKJV).

A little gossip goes a long way.

---◆•◆---

Even so the tongue is a little member and boasts great things. See how great a forest a little fire kindles! And the tongue is a fire, a world of iniquity. The tongue is so set among our members that it defiles the whole body, and sets on fire the course of nature; and it is set on fire by hell (James 3:5-6, NKJV).

A chip on the shoulder soon becomes a heavy load.

I write unto you, little children, because your sins are forgiven you for his name's sake (1 John 2:12).

The measure of a life, after all, is not its duration, but its donation. How much will you be missed?

(Peter Marshall)

———◆•◆———

For to me to live is Christ, and to die is gain (Philippians 1:21).

You can't build yourself up by tearing someone else down.

—◆•◆—

Esteem them very highly in love for their work's sake. And be in peace among yourselves (1 Thessalonians 5:13).

How we live is far more important than how long we live.

Therefore, as God's chosen people, holy and dearly loved, clothe your-selves with compassion, kindness, humility, gentleness and patience (Colossians 3:12, NIV).

Seven days without prayer make one weak.

—•◆•—

Faithful is he that calleth you, who also will do it (1 Thessalonians 5:24).

In times like these, it helps to recall that there have always been times like these.

(Paul Harvey)

A bad temper is the one thing you cannot get rid of by losing it.

A hot-tempered man stirs up dissension, but a patient man calms a quarrel (Proverbs 15:18, NIV).

Born once, die twice; born twice, die once.

Except a man be born again, he cannot see the kingdom of God (John 3:3).

Fewer words, less sin.

In the multitude of words there wanteth not sin: but he that refraineth his lips is wise (Proverbs 10:19).

A perfect faith would lift us absolutely above fear.

(George MacDonald)

Fight the good fight of faith (1 Timothy 6:12).

Some people would be completely naked if humility were their only clothing.

❖

Be clothed with humility: for God resisteth the proud, and giveth grace to the humble (1 Peter 5:5).

A hypocrite is a person who isn't himself on Sundays.

❖

And when you pray, do not be like the hypocrites, for they love to pray standing in the synagogues and on the street corners to be seen by men. I tell you the truth, they have received their reward in full (Matthew 6:5, NIV).

Don't bother to give God instructions; just report for duty.

(Corrie ten Boom)

Take care of your life; and the Lord will take care of your death.

(George Whitefield)

◆—•—◆

What is your life? It is even a vapour, that appeareth for a little time, and then vanisheth away (James 4:14).

What we love we shall grow to resemble.

(St. Bernard of Clairvaux)

He that loveth not knoweth not God; for God is love (1 John 4:8).

The true measure of loving God is to love Him without measure.

(St. Bernard of Clairvaux)

◆•◆

And you shall love the Lord your God with all your heart, with all your soul, with all your mind, and with all your strength. This is the first commandment (Mark 12:30, NKJV).

Don't let anyone use your ear as a garbage can for gossip!

And besides they learn to be idle, wandering about from house to house, and not only idle but also gossips and busybodies, saying things which they ought not (1 Timothy 5:13, NKJV).

Make all you can, save all you can, give all you can.

(John Wesley)

Give, and it shall be given unto you; good measure, pressed down, and shaken together, and running over, shall men give into your bosom. For with the same measure that ye mete withal it shall be measured to you again (Luke 6:38).

More things are wrought by prayer than this world dreams of.

(Alfred, Lord Tennyson)

———◆•◆———

Call unto me, and I will answer thee, and shew thee great and mighty things, which thou knowest not (Jeremiah 33:3).

Lamps do not talk, but they do shine.

(Charles Haddon Spurgeon)

—————◆ ● ◆—————

Let your light so shine before men, that they may see your good works, and glorify your Father which is in heaven (Matthew 5:16).

Going to church doesn't make you a Christian any more than going to a garage makes you an automobile.

(Billy Sunday)

Having a form of godliness, but denying the power thereof (2 Timothy 3:5).

To do it no more is the truest repentance.

(Martin Luther)

———◆———

Godly sorrow worketh repentance (2 Corinthians 7:10).

Service is the rent we pay for the space we occupy.

Serve the Lord with fear, and rejoice with trembling (Psalm 2:11).

The darkest night can be a blessing, if we will look for the brightest stars.

Sorrow and sighing shall flee away (Isaiah 35:10).

There is a vast difference between knowing about God and knowing Him.

———◆•◆———

Be still, and know that I am God (Psalm 46:10).

Some people who leave a temptation behind may give it a forwarding address.

Lead us not into temptation, but deliver us from evil (Matthew 6:13).

You may trust the Lord too little, but you can never trust Him too much.

God is our refuge and strength, a very present help in trouble (Psalm 46:1).

Unless we stand for some-thing, we shall fall for any-thing.

(Peter Marshall)

Therefore, my beloved brethren, be ye stedfast, unmoveable, always abounding in the work of the Lord, forasmuch as ye know that your labour is not in vain in the Lord (1 Corinthians 15:58).

Finding fault is a talent that should be buried.

Judge not, that ye be not judged (Matthew 7:1).

Fear knocked at the door.
Faith answered.
No one was there.

(Inscription at Hind's Head Inn in England).

◆•◆

Be not afraid, only believe (Mark 5:36).

If a door slams shut look for the one God is opening for you.

---◆•◆---

"For I know the plans I have for you," declares the Lord (Jeremiah 29:11, NIV).

The Bread of Life never goes stale.

I am the bread of life (John 6:35).

There is no such thing as an idle rumor; all rumors keep very busy.

———◆•◆———

Mischief shall come upon mischief, and rumour shall be upon rumour (Ezekiel 7:26).

People are as friendly as you are.

A man that hath friends must shew himself friendly (Proverbs 18:24).

Success is a relative thing. The more success you have, the more relatives you meet.

---❖•❖---

This Book of the Law shall not depart from your mouth; but you shall meditate in it day and night, that you may observe to do according to all that is written in it. For then you will make your way prosperous, and then you will have good success (Joshua 1:8, NKJV).

Laughter is life's shock absorber.

A merry heart doeth good like a medicine (Proverbs 17:22).

There are three things you can never get back once you let them go: a word spoken, a lost opportunity, a spent arrow.

That thou mayest regard discretion, and that thy lips may keep knowledge (Proverbs 5:2).

Some Christians look like they were baptized in lemon juice!

The joy of the Lord is your strength (Nehemiah 8:10).

Growing old is natural; growing up is spiritual.

Rooted and built up in him, and stablished in the faith, as ye have been taught, abounding therein with thanksgiving (Colossians 2:7).

To err is human; to remain in error is stupid.

———◆•◆———

That you put off, concerning your former conduct, the old man which grows corrupt according to the deceitful lusts, and be renewed in the spirit of your mind (Ephesians 4:22-23, NKJV).

There are three kinds of people in the world: those who make things happen, those who watch things happen and those who wonder what happened.

When you are busy rowing the boat, you don't have time to rock it.

Whatsoever thy hand findeth to do, do it with thy might (Ecclesiastes 9:10).

Breathe in God's Spirit — exhale His love.

And hope maketh not ashamed; because the love of God is shed abroad in our hearts by the Holy Ghost which is given unto us (Romans 5:5).

Don't go digging where God has buried your sins.

◆·•·◆

He will turn again, he will have compassion upon us; he will subdue our iniquities; and thou wilt cast all their sins into the depths of the sea (Micah 7:19).

Most of the things people worry about never happen.

———◆•◆———

Be anxious for nothing, but in everything by prayer and supplication, with thanksgiving, let your requests be made known to God; and the peace of God, which surpasses all understanding, will guard your hearts and minds through Christ Jesus (Philippians 4:6-7, NKJV).

Keep your words soft and sweet. You may have to eat them!

Let your speech always be with grace, seasoned with salt, that you may know how you ought to answer each one (Colossians 4:6, NKJV).

There is never a final good-bye among loved ones who know Jesus.

But I would not have you to be ignorant, brethren, concerning them which are asleep, that ye sorrow not, even as others which have no hope (1 Thessalonians 4:13).

Don't let your get-up-and-go get up and go.

Whatsoever ye do, do it heartily, as to the Lord, and not unto men (Colossians 3:23).

It's not how old you are that counts, but how you are old.

I have been young, and now am old; yet have I not seen the righteous forsaken (Psalm 37:25).

Anger is a wind which blows out the lamp of the mind.

(Robert Ingersoll)

He that is slow to anger is better than the mighty (Proverbs 16:32).

Character is what you are in the dark.

(D.L. Moody)

Even a child is known by his doings (Proverbs 20:11).

A camel is a race horse that was put together by a committee!

———◆•◆———

Many are the plans in a man's heart, but it is the Lord's purpose that prevails (Proverbs 19:20, NIV).

When you were born, you cried and everyone else was happy. Live your life in such a way that when you die, you will be happy and everyone else will cry.

This present moment is all the time you can be sure of.

Now is the accepted time; behold, now is the day of salvation (2 Corinthians 6:2).

In three days, guests, like fish, begin to stink.

(Benjamin Franklin)

———◆•◆———

Withdraw thy foot from thy neighbour's house; lest he be weary of thee, and so hate thee (Proverbs 25:17).

The door to happiness opens outward.

(Soren Kierkegaard)

❖

Love worketh no ill to his neighbour (Romans 13:10).

How it improves people for us when we begin to love them.

(David Grayson)

---❖---

Beloved, if God so loved us, we ought also to love one another (1 John 4:11).

We grow too soon old and too late schmart.

(Pennsylvania Dutch saying)

❖

For the Lord giveth wisdom: out of his mouth cometh knowledge and understanding (Proverbs 2:6).

No one can make you feel inferior without your consent.

(Eleanor Roosevelt)

But we have this treasure in earthen vessels, that the excellency of the power may be of God, and not of us (2 Corinthians 4:7).

It's easier to do a good job than to explain why you didn't.

And whatever you do in word or deed, do all in the name of the Lord Jesus, giving thanks to God the Father through Him (Colossians 3:17, NKJV).

The worst liars in the world are your own fears.

———◆•◆———

Fear not, little flock; for it is your Father's good pleasure to give you the kingdom (Luke 12:32).

When down in the mouth remember Jonah — he came out all right!

(Thomas A. Edison)

For in Jesus Christ neither circumcision availeth any thing, nor uncircumcision; but faith which worketh by love (Galatians 5:6).

Diamonds are chunks of coal that stuck to their job while under pressure.

—•◆•—

Keep thy heart with all diligence; for out of it are the issues of life (Proverbs 4:23).

Lord, when we are wrong, make us willing to change. And when we are right, make us easy to live with.

(Peter Marshall)

———◆•◆———

God resists the proud, But gives grace to the humble (1 Peter 5:5, NKJV).

Do not worry about what people are thinking about you — for they are not thinking about you. They are wondering what you are thinking about them.

(Anonymous)

The best way out is always through.

(Robert Frost)

God is faithful, who will not suffer you to be tempted above that ye are able; but will with the temptation also make a way to escape, that ye may be able to bear it (1 Corinthians 10:13).

You don't learn much when you are talking.

Be still, and know that I am God (Psalm 46:10).

Learn to distinguish between your needs and your wants.

But my God shall supply all your need according to his riches in glory by Christ Jesus (Philippians 4:19).

The night is always darkest right before the dawn.

Thou hast turned for me my mourning into dancing: thou hast put off my sackcloth, and girded me with gladness (Psalm 30:11).

Faith is not merely you holding on to God — it is God holding on to you.

(E. Stanley Jones)

❖

Have faith in God (Mark 11:22).

Faith is something that has to be applied.

(Corrie ten Boom)

Thus also faith by itself, if it does not have works, is dead (James 2:17, NKJV).

We are to take care of the possible and let God take care of the impossible.

(Ruth Bell Graham)

◆•◆

All things are possible to him that believeth (Mark 9:23).

When is the last time you did a random act of kindness?

◆•◆

Therefore, as God's chosen people, holy and dearly loved, clothe your-selves with compassion, kindness, humility, gentleness and patience (Colossians 3:12, NIV).

Sympathy is two hearts tugging at the same load.

❖•❖

Carry each others burdens, and in this way you will fulfill the law of Christ (Galatians 6:2, NIV).

Don't laugh at those who fall; there may be some slippery places in your own life.

—◆•◆—

Brothers, if someone is caught in a sin, you who are spiritual should restore him gently. But watch yourself, or you also may be tempted (Galatians 6:1).

What will people say about you after you are gone?

---◆•◆---

A good name is rather to be chosen than great riches, and loving favour rather than silver and gold (Proverbs 22:1).

A good conscience is a continual Christmas.

(Benjamin Franklin)

———◆●◆———

There is therefore now no condemnation to them which are in Christ Jesus, who walk not after the flesh, but after the Spirit (Romans 8:1).

Truth is stranger than fiction, but not quite as popular!

The truth shall make you free (John 8:32).

Don't lose your head — your brain is in it!

———◆•◆———

Teach us to number our days, that we may apply our hearts unto wisdom (Psalm 90:12).

How old is your attitude?

◆•◆

Even to your old age I am He (Isaiah 46:4).

Let God lift you up, and you won't let yourself down.

He brought me up also out of an horrible pit, out of the miry clay, and set my feet upon a rock, and established my goings (Psalm 40:2).

If you worry about what might be and wonder about what might have been, you will miss what is.

———◆•◆———

Therefore do not worry about tomorrow, for tomorrow will worry about itself. Each day has enough trouble of its own (Matthew 6:34).

Prayer is a cry of distress, a demand for help, a hymn of love.

Pray without ceasing (1 Thessalonians 5:17).

When pain is to be borne, a little courage helps more than much knowledge.

(C.S. Lewis)

Be strong and of a good courage (Joshua 1:6).

Lying in bed paralyzed, I learned two things: Tolerance and patience toward myself and everyone else.

(Roy Campanella)

———◆•◆———

Rest in the Lord, and wait patiently for him (Psalm 37:7).

People should always give more consideration to how much they have rather than to how much they want.

In every thing give thanks: for this is the will of God in Christ Jesus concerning you (1 Thessalonians 5:18).

When you find yourself in a hole, stop digging!

I will lift up mine eyes unto the hills, from whence cometh my help. My help cometh from the Lord, which made heaven and earth (Psalm 121:1-2).

It takes more muscles to frown than it does to smile.

A merry heart maketh a cheerful countenance (Proverbs 15:13).

It is better to wear out than to rust out.

(G. Horne)

———◆•◆———

Therefore, my dear brothers, stand firm. Let nothing move you.
Always give yourselves fully to the work of the Lord, because you
know that your labor in the Lord is not in vain
(1 Corinthians 15:58, NIV).

Sleep is sweet to the labouring man.

(John Bunyan)

For so he giveth his beloved sleep (Psalm 127:2).

Inside every seventy-year-old is a thirty-five-year-old asking: "What happened?"

(Ann Landers)

Therefore we do not lose heart. Though outwardly we are wasting away, yet inwardly we are being renewed day by day (2 Corinthians 4:16, NIV).